STAR WARS
EMPIRE

VOLUME THREE: THE IMPERIAL PERSPECTIVE

THIS STORY TAKES PLACE DURING
AND SHORTLY AFTER THE EVENTS
IN STAR WARS: A NEW HOPE.

STAR WARS: EMPIRE VOLUME 3

THIS VOLUME COLLECTS ISSUES #13, 14 AND #16-
19 OF THE COMIC-BOOK SERIES STAR WARS: EMPIRE.

PUBLISHED BY
DARK HORSE BOOKS
A DIVISION OF DARK HORSE COMICS, INC.
10956 SE MAIN STREET
MILWAUKIE, OR 97222

WWW.DARKHORSE.COM
WWW.STARWARS.COM

TO FIND A COMICS SHOP IN YOUR
AREA, CALL THE COMIC SHOP
LOCATOR SERVICE TOLL-FREE
AT 1-888-266-4226

FIRST EDITION: OCTOBER 2004
ISBN: 1-59307-128-0

3 5 7 9 10 8 6 4 2

PRINTED IN CHINA

VOLUME THREE:
THE IMPERIAL PERSPECTIVE

WRITERS PAUL ALDEN
JEREMY BARLOW
WELLES HARTLEY
RON MARZ

ARTISTS PATRICK BLAINE
BRIAN CHING
DAVIDÉ FABBRI
& CHRISTIAN DALLA VECCHIA
RAUL TREVINO

COLORISTS MICHAEL ATIYEH
DAVIDÉ FABBRI
RAUL TREVINO
STUDIO F

LETTERERS SNO CONE STUDIOS
MICHAEL DAVID THOMAS

FRONT COVER ART BY DOUG WHEATLEY

BACK COVER ART BY DAVID MICHAEL BECK
& BRAD ANDERSON

STAR WARS®
EMPIRE

PUBLISHER
MIKE RICHARDSON

COLLECTION DESIGNER
LANI SCHREIBSTEIN

ART DIRECTOR
LIA RIBACCHI

ASSOCIATE EDITOR
JEREMY BARLOW

EDITOR
RANDY STRADLEY

SPECIAL THANKS TO
SUE ROSTONI, AMY GARY,
CHRIS CERASI, AND LUCY AUTREY WILSON
AT LUCAS LICENSING

DAVID MICHAEL BECK
COLORS BRAD ANDERSON

WHAT SIN LOYALTY?

Script JEREMY BARLOW
Art PATRICK BLAINE
Colors STUDIO F

THE PLANET *RALLTIIR*. FOUR DAYS PRIOR TO THE BATTLE OF YAVIN.

IT WASN'T SUPPOSED TO GO DOWN LIKE THIS.

WE EXPECTED *SOME* RESISTANCE, OF COURSE, AND WE CAME READY FOR A FIGHT. BUT NO ONE WAS PREPARED FOR HOW DEEPLY THE FANATICISM RAN.

THAT SMALL, EXPLOSIVE VOICE THAT'S SPREADING ACROSS THE GALAXY HAD REACHED RALLTIIR A LONG TIME AGO, WHISPERING WORDS OF ANARCHY AND CHAOS...

KZAAT
KZAAT

...AND BY THE TIME WE ARRIVED HERE, THOSE WHISPERS HAD BECOME A *ROAR*.

TAKE HIM *OUT!*

THAT VOICE WANTS TO SHAKE THE EMPIRE'S FOUNDATION. TO CRUMBLE THE *ORDER* BUILT FROM THE ASHES OF THE CLONE WARS.

ZING

BUT THAT WON'T HAPPEN. NO MATTER HOW MANY SMALL STRIKES THEY MAKE, NO MATTER HOW MANY PLANETS THEY *INFECT*, NO MATTER HOW HARD THEY TRY...

SIR? WE WERE SENT HERE TO HELP THESE PEOPLE SHAKE THE ALLIANCE'S CONTROL, AND THEY THANK US BY POINTING GUNS AT OUR BACKS AND HIDING DETONATORS UNDER OUR BEDS.

NOT EVERYONE THINKS WE'RE HERE TO HELP. TO SOME, WE'RE *OCCUPIERS*, NOT LIBERATORS. I GREW UP HERE, REMEMBER. I WATCHED THE POLITICAL LANDSCAPE CHANGE. REBEL SENTIMENT RUNS DEEP. IT'LL TAKE YEARS TO WASH IT AWAY.

YOU'RE A GOOD SOLDIER, 622. ALWAYS ON YOUR GUARD, WHETHER THE SITUATION WARRANTS IT OR NOT.

THAT'S WHAT I WAS CREATED FOR. I LIKE TO THINK THAT I LIVE UP TO MY STATION.

AND THEN SOME.

BUT WE WON'T HAVE TO WORRY ABOUT RALLTIIR FOR TOO MUCH LONGER. THE ENTIRE DIVISION IS BEING ROTATED OUT TOMORROW. REASSIGNED TO THE NEW IMPERIAL BATTLE STATION.

REASSIGNED? WE HAVEN'T COMPLETED OUR MISSION HERE YET.

DEET DEET DEET

BLAST!

I DON'T KNOW IF THIS MISSION *CAN* BE COMPLETED. I WANTED TO SAVE MY HOME WORLD, BUT MY JUDGMENT'S BECOME CLOUDED, AND I DON'T WANT THAT TO PUT ANYONE ELSE IN JEOPARDY. ESPECIALLY AFTER WHAT HAPPENED THE OTHER NIGHT.

DON'T WORRY, I'M SURE YOU'LL FIND PLENTY OF ACTION ABOARD THE NEW BATTLE STATION --

WAIT! DO YOU HEAR THAT?

DEET DEET DEET

GET DOWN -- *NOW!*

"MAYBE YOU'LL FIND SOMETHING WE CAN USE TO BUILD A CASE FOR SCRAPPING THESE THINGS."

THAT'S A NEW ONE. SO, WHO'D THIS DROID TRY TO FRY, ANYWAY? I HOPE IT WASN'T TARKIN. THOUGH IF IT WERE, I'D BE IMPRESSED WITH ITS --

I TELL YOU, THESE DROIDS ARE JUNK. THEY WERE MADE CHEAP TO BEGIN WITH, GIVEN OUT AS "GIFTS" TO ALL THE HIGH-RANKING IMPERIAL BUREAUCRATS. SOMEHOW ALMOST THE ENTIRE PRODUCTION RUN ENDED UP ON THIS STATION.

IT TRIED TO KILL SOME OFFICERS ON C DECK.

WHAT'D THIS ONE DO, LOCK YOU IN THE REFRESHER?

IT WAS COMMANDER AKOBI. IS IT POSSIBLE THIS DROID'S PROGRAMMING WAS ALTERED?

NOT LIKELY. THESE THINGS HAVE FUSED PROCESSORS --

-- IT'S ONE OF THE REASONS THEY'RE SO DUMB, THEY CAN'T BE UPGRADED AND THEY CAN'T THINK OUTSIDE OF THEIR DIRECTIVES.

KINDA LIKE CLONES. NO OFFENSE.

IS THERE ANY WAY TO SLOW THIS FEED DOWN? I CAN HARDLY READ IT.

NOPE, THIS IS IT. ANOTHER DESIGN FLAW.

AKOBI JUST TRANSFERRED FROM RALLTIIR, RIGHT? I'VE HEARD STORIES ABOUT THAT GUY. NASTY THINGS. LIKE HE TORCHED A BUNCH OF WOMEN AND CHILDREN --

WHATEVER YOU HEARD IS A LIE... WAIT, GO BACK! I SAW SOMETHING!

ZZZAAK

WHO HAS ACCESS TO THESE DROIDS' PROGRAMMING?

WHY? WHAT'D YOU SEE?

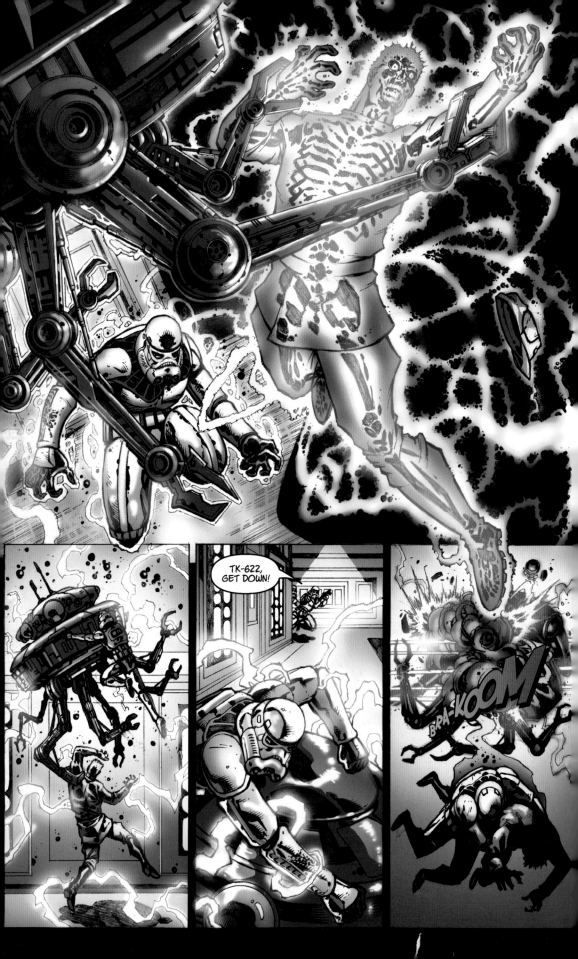

UNLIKE MY OWN, AKOBI'S WOUNDS ARE TERMINAL. HE'S NOT EXPECTED TO LAST THROUGH THE NIGHT.

THERE *IS* A SABOTEUR ABOARD; THAT MUCH IS CLEAR. BUT WITHOUT PROOF, I'M ON MY OWN. AND WITHOUT AKOBI'S DIRECTION...

...ALL I CAN DO IS RETRACE THE STEPS...

...KEEP ASKING QUESTIONS, AVOID DISTRACTION ... AND HOPE THAT LEADS ME *SOMEWHERE*.

BASED ON THE SERIAL INFO, I'D SAY THIS THING CAME FROM NEAR THE EQUATORIAL TRENCH. WOULDN'T HURT TO TAKE A LOOK DOWN THERE...

IT TOOK HALF A DAY TO GET DOWN THERE. IT WAS DIFFICULT TO STAY FOCUSED.

WHICH MADE THE TIMING FOR A REBEL INVASION ALL THE WORSE.

EVERY OFFICER I ENCOUNTERED POTENTIALLY THREATENED MY COURSE -- EVEN THE SLIGHTEST ORDER MIGHT ALTER MY DIRECTION OR THROW ME OFF TRACK.

NO TELLING HOW MANY CAME ABOARD...

...OR *WHO* OR *WHAT* THEY LEFT BEHIND.

FUSED PROCESSORS? WHO TOLD YOU THAT? RA-7'S ARE A CINCH TO REWIRE. THAT'S WHY THEY'RE SO DUMB...

...ENDING UP WHERE I BEGAN. WHERE DOES THE TRAIL LEAD?

IF AKOBI DIES, THAT TRAIL GROWS COLD. AND NOT ONLY WILL I LOSE ANY HOPE OF FINDING WHO'S BEHIND THIS...

I'M GOING IN CIRCLES...

...BUT I'LL ALSO LOSE MY ONLY FRIEND.

-- AS WELL AS FROM WITHOUT.

AND IN MY MOMENT OF DOUBT, WE FALL. JUST LIKE THAT, IT'S ALL OVER.

THE SAVAGE HEART

SCRIPT PAUL ALDEN
ART RAUL TREVINO

THE BATTLE OF YAVIN.

ANGER. IT IS THE ONE EMOTION THAT *DARTH VADER* FEELS THE STRONGEST. AND AT THIS MOMENT IT IS AT ITS *PEAK.*

BUT A *TRUE SITH* UNDERSTANDS ANGER. KNOWS HOW TO *HARNESS* IT -- AND *BEND IT* TO HIS WILL.

IT IS *THIS* ABILITY THAT ALLOWS VADER TO REGAIN CONTROL OF HIS CRIPPLED VESSEL AND ESCAPE INTO THE BLACKNESS OF SPACE...

...THOUGH THE DAMAGE HIS SHIP HAS SUSTAINED HAS KNOCKED OUT COMMUNICATIONS...

...AND LIMITED ITS *HYPERSPACE* NAVIGATION CAPABILITIES.

THERE IS ONLY ONE IMPERIAL OUTPOST WITHIN VADER'S REACH.

RAGE HAS BEEN TRANSFORMED INTO POWER. REVENGE WILL HAVE ITS DAY.

FOR NOW, VADER'S THOUGHTS TURN TOWARD SURVIVAL...

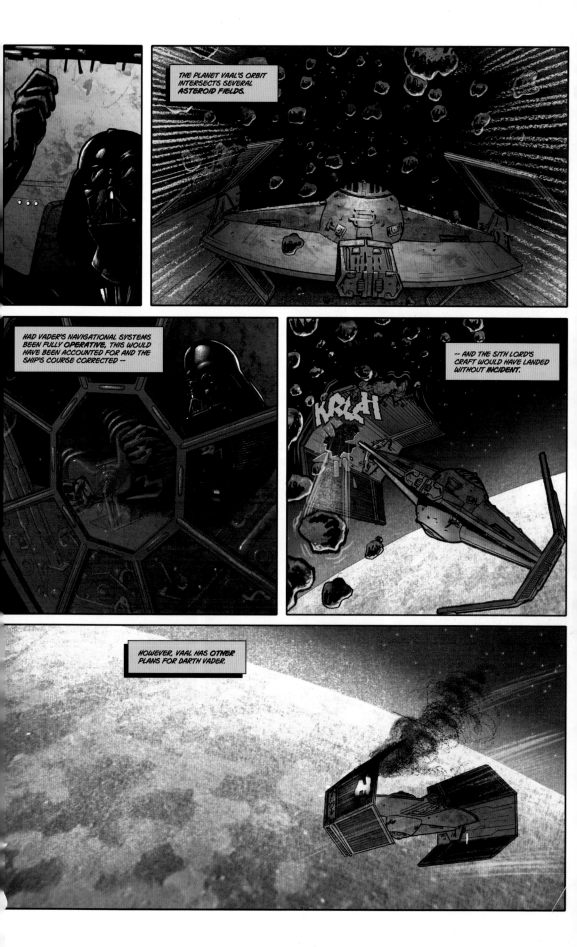

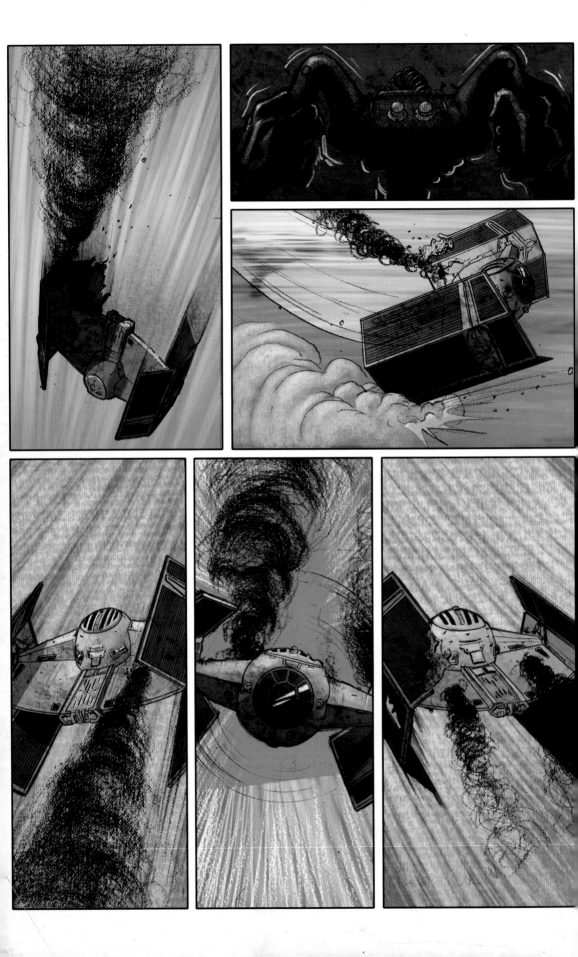

SNRRAARG!

EVEN HERE THERE ARE LEADERS, AND FOLLOWERS.

HAVING TAKEN THE LIFE OF ONE OF VAAL'S MOST VICIOUS LEADERS, A STRANGE FEELING COMES OVER VADER...

BEYOND HIS LIFE-SUSTAINING MACHINERY AND MILITARISTIC DISCIPLINE, VADER FEELS AN EXHILARATING RUSH OF JOY.

AND FOR THE FIRST TIME IN YEARS, HE FEELS TRULY ALIVE.

VMMMM

THE IMPERIAL OUTPOST IS NEAR. VADER COULD REACH IT BY MID-MORNING. BUT INSTEAD HE PAUSES, HOPING TO PROLONG THE FEELING THAT HAS ENVELOPED HIM...

...AND HE SENSES THAT VAAL IS NOT FINISHED WITH HIM YET.

MORNING COMES TOO QUICKLY --

-- AND WITH IT A REMINDER OF VADER'S LIFELONG COMPANION... *FEAR.*

BUT FEAR GIVES WAY TO ANOTHER EMOTION...

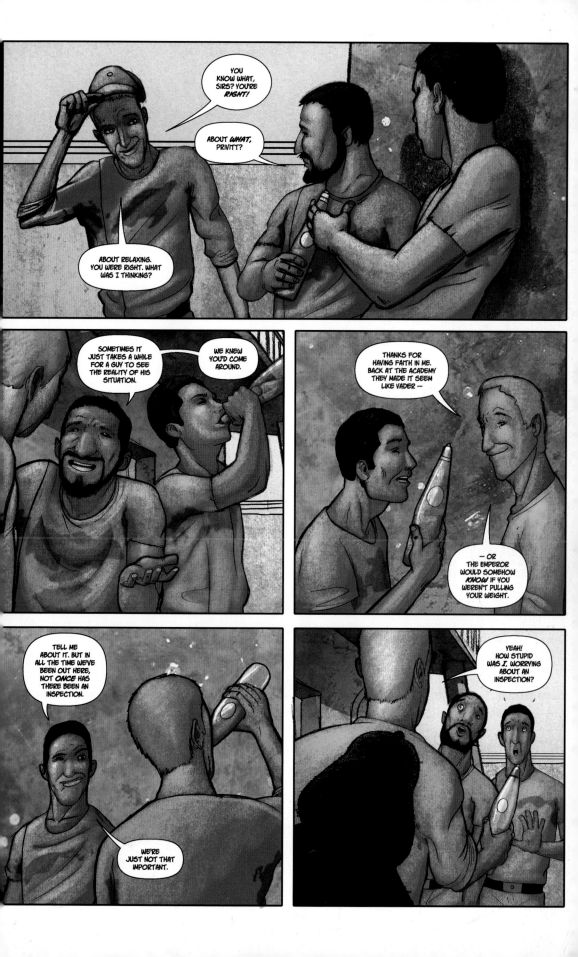

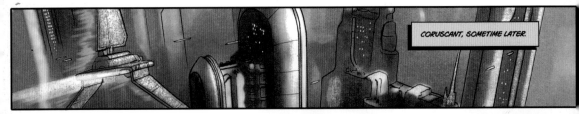

CORUSCANT, SOMETIME LATER.

INFORM THE EMPEROR OF MY ARRIVAL AND DISPATCH A CREW TO RETRIEVE MY FIGHTER FROM THE PLANET VAAL.

LORD VADER! WE WERE MOST PLEASED TO LEARN YOU ESCAPED THE *INCIDENT* AT YAVIN. SOME HAD FEARED THE WORST...

TELL THEM TO TREAT IT AS THOUGH IT IS WORTH THEIR *LIVES.*

DISPATCH A NEW RELAY TEAM TO VAAL, AS WELL. THEY WILL FIND THAT THE STATION IS CURRENTLY UNMANNED.

I WILL BE IN MY QUARTERS, COMMANDER. I AM *NOT* TO BE DISTURBED.

END

TO THE LAST MAN

Script WELLES HARTLEY
Pencils and colors DAVIDÉ FABBRI
Inks CHRISTIAN DALLA VECCHIA

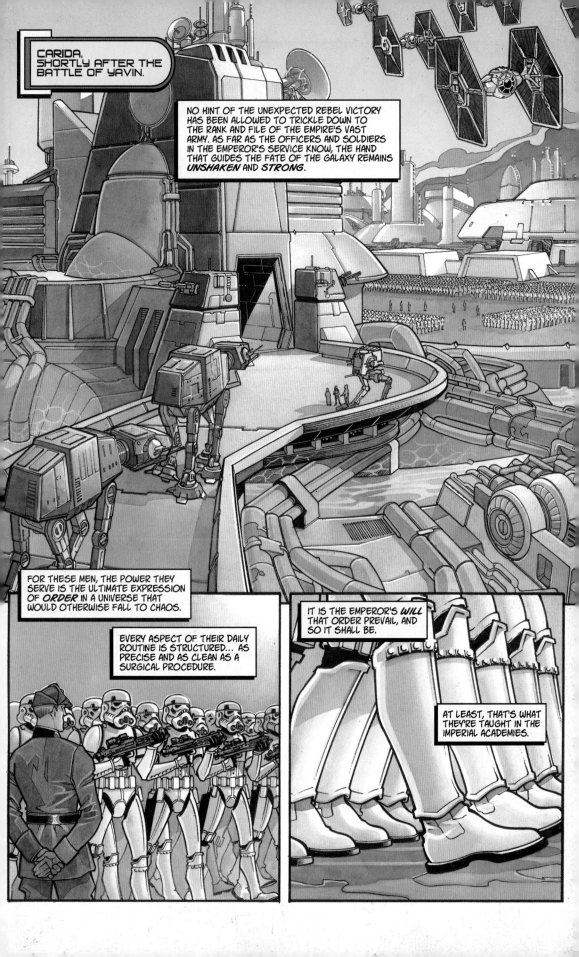

CARIDA, SHORTLY AFTER THE BATTLE OF YAVIN.

NO HINT OF THE UNEXPECTED REBEL VICTORY HAS BEEN ALLOWED TO TRICKLE DOWN TO THE RANK AND FILE OF THE EMPIRE'S VAST ARMY. AS FAR AS THE OFFICERS AND SOLDIERS IN THE EMPEROR'S SERVICE KNOW, THE HAND THAT GUIDES THE FATE OF THE GALAXY REMAINS *UNSHAKEN* AND *STRONG*.

FOR THESE MEN, THE POWER THEY SERVE IS THE ULTIMATE EXPRESSION OF *ORDER* IN A UNIVERSE THAT WOULD OTHERWISE FALL TO CHAOS.

EVERY ASPECT OF THEIR DAILY ROUTINE IS STRUCTURED... AS PRECISE AND AS CLEAN AS A SURGICAL PROCEDURE.

IT IS THE EMPEROR'S *WILL* THAT ORDER PREVAIL, AND SO IT SHALL BE.

AT LEAST, THAT'S WHAT THEY'RE TAUGHT IN THE IMPERIAL ACADEMIES.

MARIDUN, A JUNGLE WORLD.

...AS *LT. JANEK SUNBER* HAS DISCOVERED.

BUT THEN, THAT'S JUST *ONE MORE* PIECE OF SUNBER'S LIFE THAT HAS TURNED OUT DIFFERENTLY THAN HE'D ANTICIPATED.

IN *PRACTICE*, THINGS ARE RARELY AS ELEGANT AS THEY ARE IN *THEORY*...

HE HAD HOPED TO BE A PILOT... ONE OF THE GLAMOUR BOYS OF THE EMPIRE... BUT, THOUGH HE IS AN ABOVE AVERAGE PILOT, HIS SKILLS ARE NOT UP TO IMPERIAL STANDARDS.

RATHER THAN FACE THE HUMILIATION OF RETURNING HOME A FAILURE, HE HAS OPTED FOR THE INFANTRY. HE IS SURE HIS FRIENDS... WHO PLANNED TO *FOLLOW* HIM TO THE ACADEMY... WOULDN'T UNDERSTAND... JUST AS HE IS SURE THAT *THEY* WILL MAKE *GREAT* PILOTS.

BUT THE ROUTE HE HAS CHOSEN HAS GIVEN HIM DISCIPLINE AND SELF-RESPECT, AND HE IS SURE THAT IT WILL... *EVENTUALLY*... PROVIDE HIM WITH A RESPECTED POSITION WITHIN THE EMPIRE *AND* SOCIETY... SOMETHING HE COULD NEVER HOPE FOR BACK HOME.

HIS DEDICATION TO THE EMPEROR'S SERVICE HAS PAID OFF... HE HAS MADE OFFICER RANK IN LESS THAN A YEAR. IT HAS BEEN HARD, DIRTY WORK, BUT HE COUNTS IT AS WORTHWHILE.

STILL, NOT A DAY GOES BY THAT HE DOESN'T THINK OF HIS FRIENDS, AND THE *EASIER* PATH THEY MUST HAVE.

THAT'S IT, SUNBER. KEEP YOUR MEN MOVING.

DON'T FALL BEHIND NOW.

YES, SIR, *CAPTAIN GAGE*.

LIEUTENANT SUNBER, *COME HERE.*

SIR?

WHAT DO YOU *THINK* YOU'RE DOING, SUNBER?

HELPING MY MEN, SIR...

YOUR JOB IS TO *DIRECT* YOUR MEN... NOT DIRTY YOUR HANDS WITH THEIR TOIL.

AS AN OFFICER, YOU SHOULD BE *BETTER* THAN THIS... *REGARDLESS* OF YOUR *ACTUAL* BACKGROUND. NOW, GET THIS VEHICLE MOVING!

SUNBER RANKLES FROM GAGE'S CHASTISEMENT. GAGE HAS MADE A CAREER OUT OF PUTTING FORTH THE LEAST AMOUNT OF EFFORT POSSIBLE...

...BUT SUNBER KNOWS THAT *ALL* DUTY IS SACRIFICE...

... AND IN THE EMPEROR'S SERVICE, THE SACRIFICE OF SWEAT IS THE *LEAST* THAT COULD BE ASKED OF HIM.

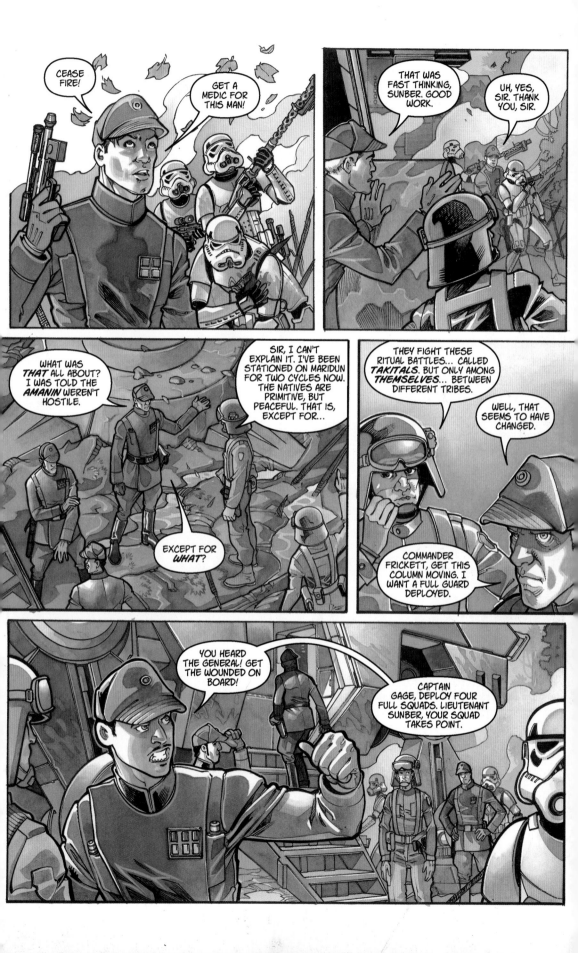

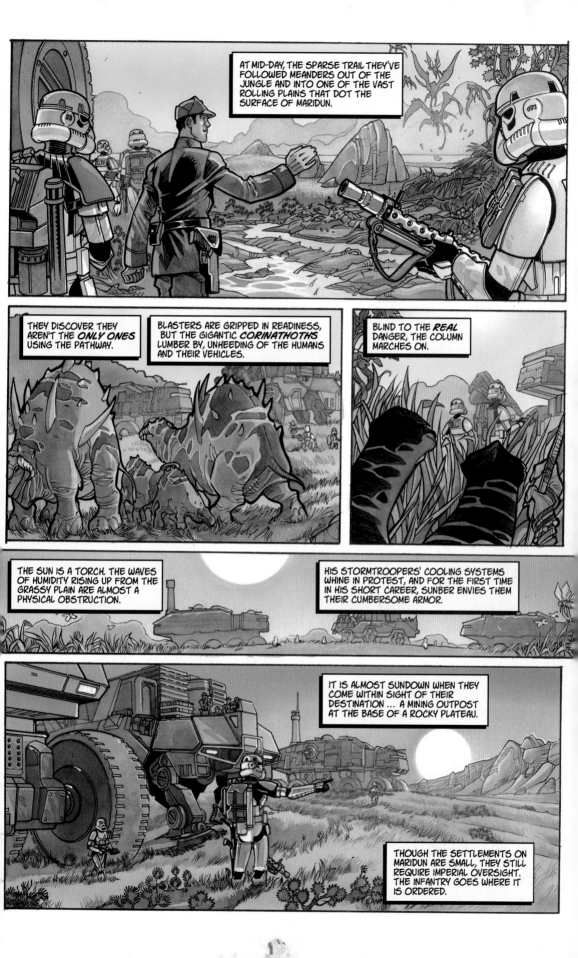

AT MID-DAY, THE SPARSE TRAIL THEY'VE FOLLOWED MEANDERS OUT OF THE JUNGLE AND INTO ONE OF THE VAST ROLLING PLAINS THAT DOT THE SURFACE OF MARIDUN.

THEY DISCOVER THEY AREN'T THE *ONLY ONES* USING THE PATHWAY.

BLASTERS ARE GRIPPED IN READINESS, BUT THE GIGANTIC *CORINATHOTHS* LUMBER BY, UNHEEDING OF THE HUMANS AND THEIR VEHICLES.

BLIND TO THE *REAL* DANGER, THE COLUMN MARCHES ON.

THE SUN IS A TORCH. THE WAVES OF HUMIDITY RISING UP FROM THE GRASSY PLAIN ARE ALMOST A PHYSICAL OBSTRUCTION.

HIS STORMTROOPERS' COOLING SYSTEMS WHINE IN PROTEST, AND FOR THE FIRST TIME IN HIS SHORT CAREER, SUNBER ENVIES THEM THEIR CUMBERSOME ARMOR.

IT IS ALMOST SUNDOWN WHEN THEY COME WITHIN SIGHT OF THEIR DESTINATION ... A MINING OUTPOST AT THE BASE OF A ROCKY PLATEAU.

THOUGH THE SETTLEMENTS ON MARIDUN ARE SMALL, THEY STILL REQUIRE IMPERIAL OVERSIGHT. THE INFANTRY GOES WHERE IT IS ORDERED.

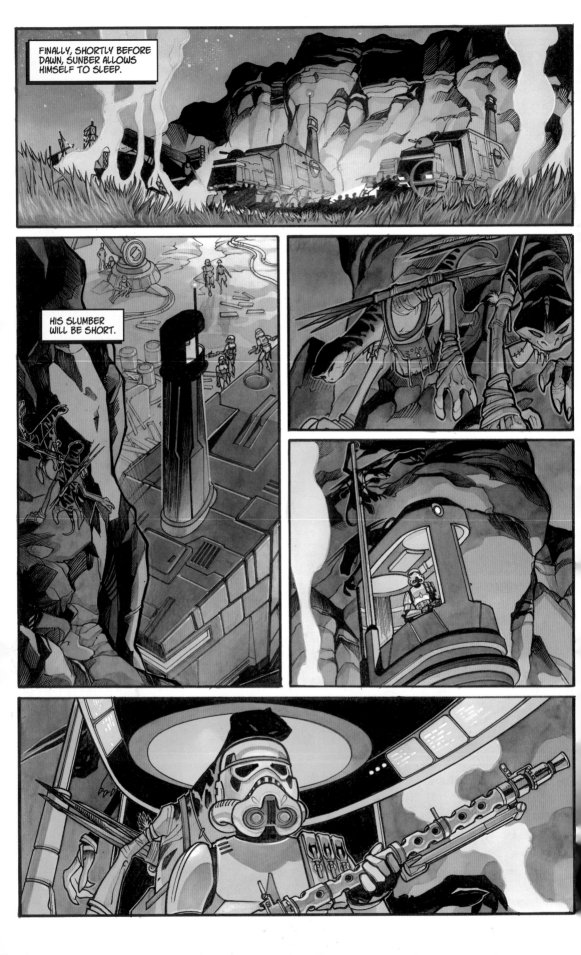

FINALLY, SHORTLY BEFORE DAWN, SUNBER ALLOWS HIMSELF TO SLEEP.

HIS SLUMBER WILL BE SHORT.

IT IS ONE OF THOSE MOMENTS THAT BURNS ITSELF INTO THE MEMORY. IN RAPID SUCCESSION, THE MEN IN GENERAL ZIERING'S COMPANY EXPERIENCE SHOCK, BEWILDERMENT, AND FEAR.

IT IS A SIGHT THAT NUMBS THE RESPONSES, AND DRIVES ACADEMY-LEARNED LESSONS FROM OFFICERS' MINDS.

FOR A MOMENT... OR AN AGE... NOTHING HAPPENS. THE EMPIRE'S BEST AND BRIGHTEST JUST STAND AND STARE...

IT'S MADNESS, BUT SUNBER SEEMS TO BE THE ONLY ONE TO REALIZE IT. THE ALIENS ARE AT THE EXTREME EDGE OF A BLASTER RIFLE'S EFFECTIVE RANGE. SHOOTING AT THEM IS A FUTILE GESTURE AT BEST...

...A WASTE OF PRECIOUS AMMUNITION AT WORST.

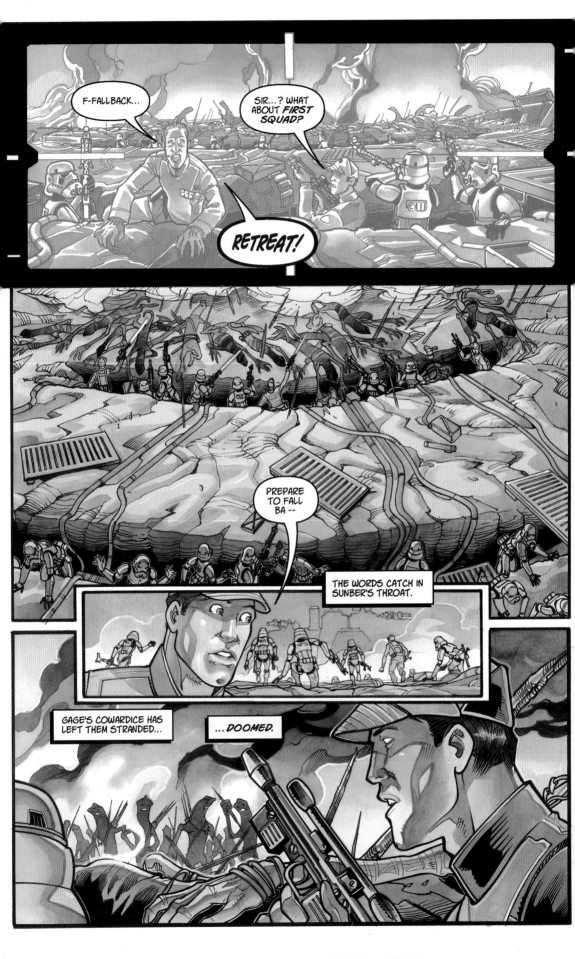

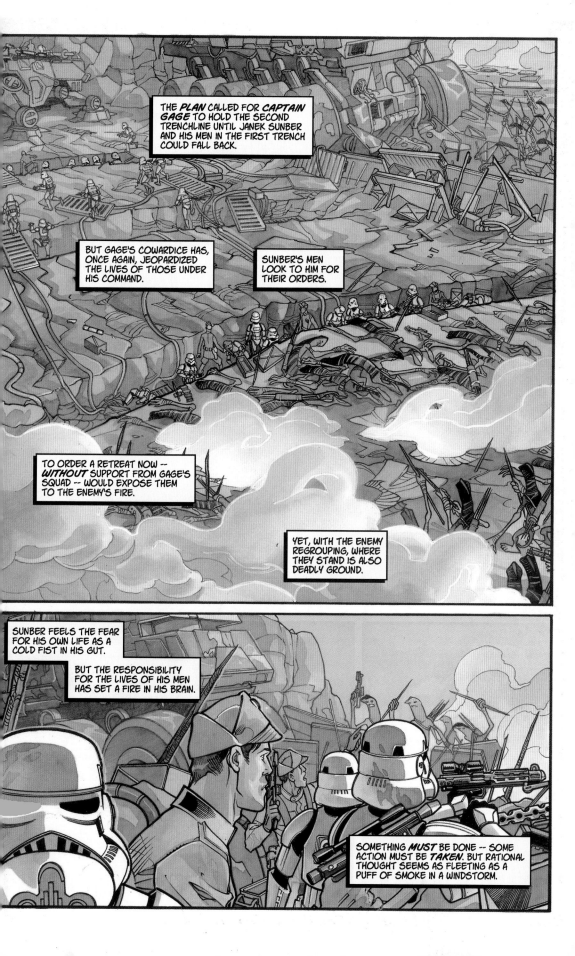

THE *PLAN* CALLED FOR *CAPTAIN GAGE* TO HOLD THE SECOND TRENCHLINE UNTIL JANEK SUNBER AND HIS MEN IN THE FIRST TRENCH COULD FALL BACK.

BUT GAGE'S COWARDICE HAS, ONCE AGAIN, JEOPARDIZED THE LIVES OF THOSE UNDER HIS COMMAND.

SUNBER'S MEN LOOK TO HIM FOR THEIR ORDERS.

TO ORDER A RETREAT NOW -- *WITHOUT* SUPPORT FROM GAGE'S SQUAD -- WOULD EXPOSE THEM TO THE ENEMY'S FIRE.

YET, WITH THE ENEMY REGROUPING, WHERE THEY STAND IS ALSO DEADLY GROUND.

SUNBER FEELS THE FEAR FOR HIS OWN LIFE AS A COLD FIST IN HIS GUT.

BUT THE RESPONSIBILITY FOR THE LIVES OF HIS MEN HAS SET A FIRE IN HIS BRAIN.

SOMETHING *MUST* BE DONE -- SOME ACTION MUST BE *TAKEN*. BUT RATIONAL THOUGHT SEEMS AS FLEETING AS A PUFF OF SMOKE IN A WINDSTORM.

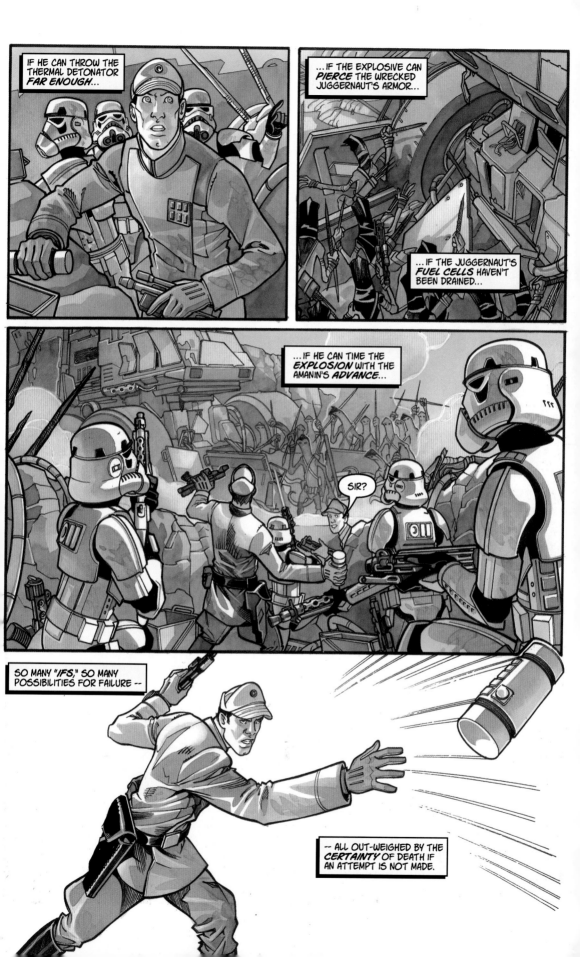

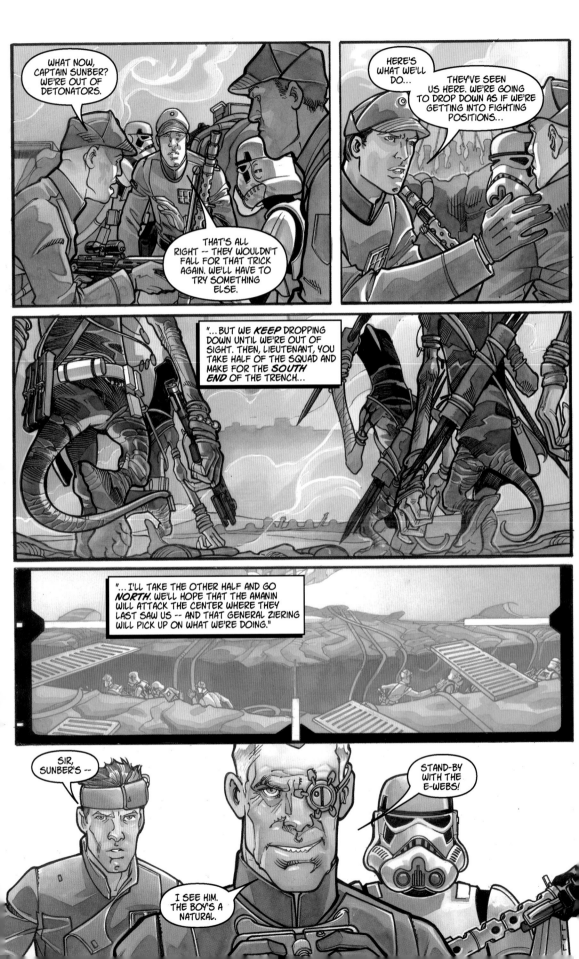

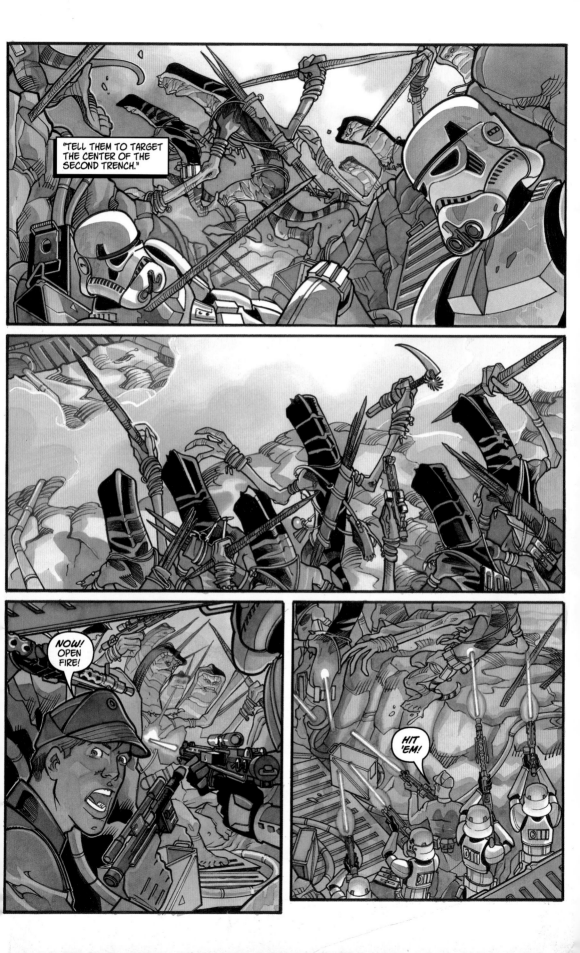

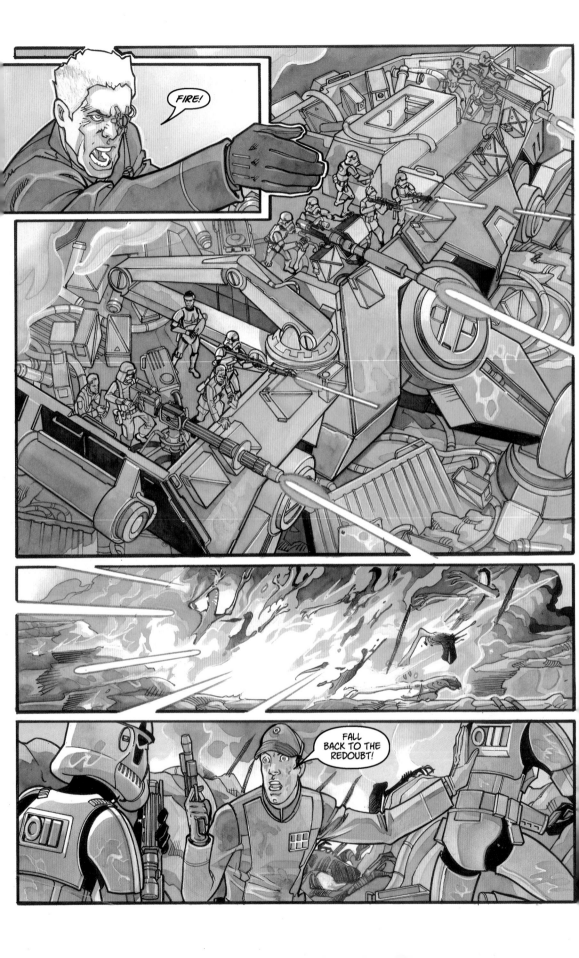

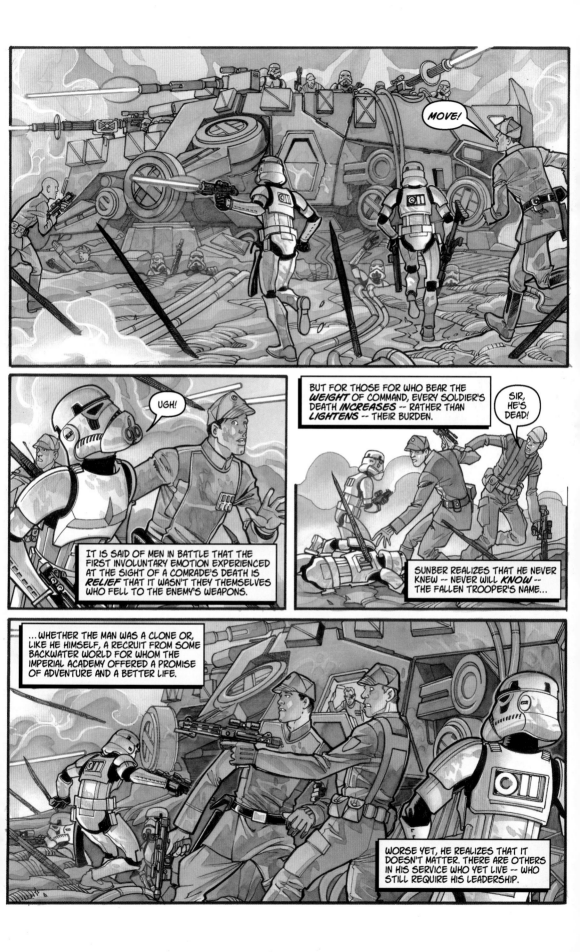

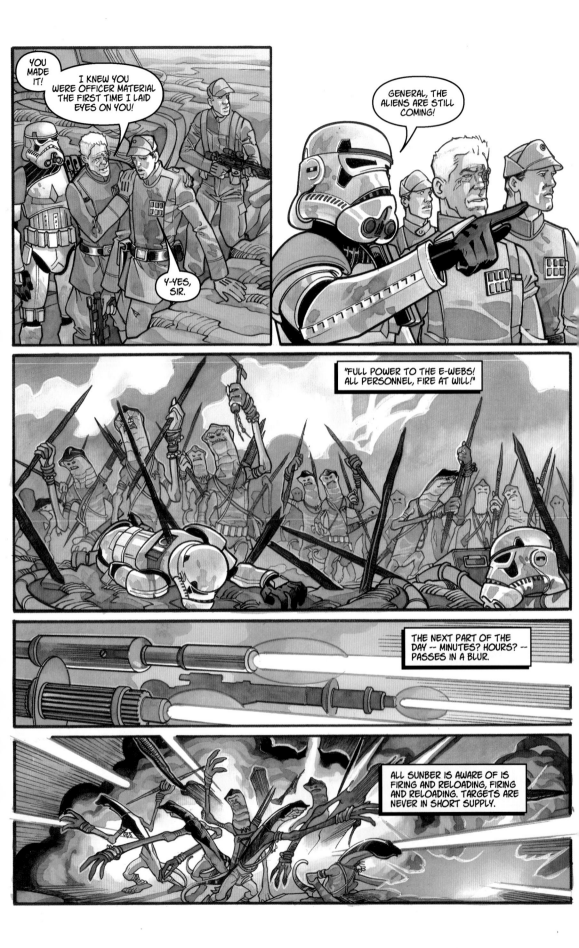

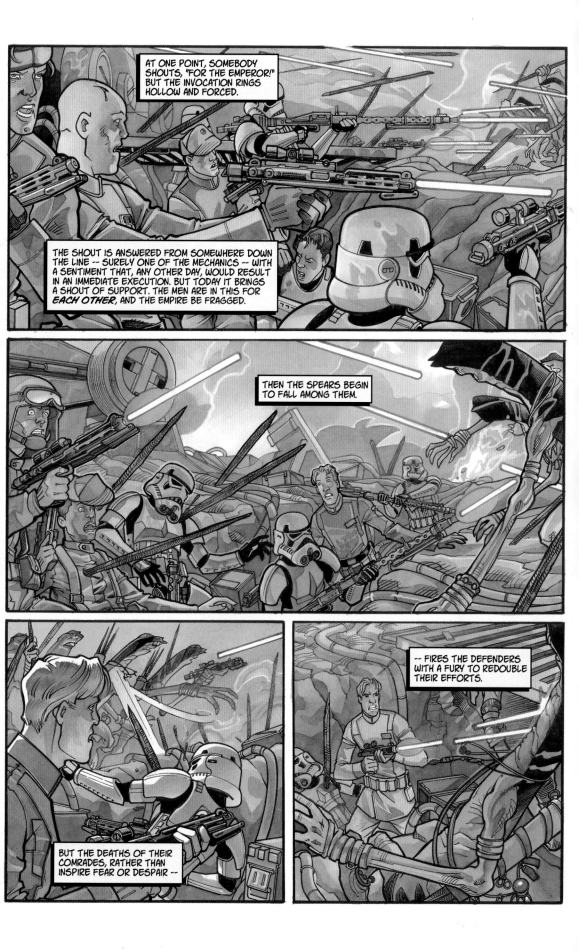

AT ONE POINT, SOMEBODY SHOUTS, "FOR THE EMPEROR!" BUT THE INVOCATION RINGS HOLLOW AND FORCED.

THE SHOUT IS ANSWERED FROM SOMEWHERE DOWN THE LINE -- SURELY ONE OF THE MECHANICS -- WITH A SENTIMENT THAT, ANY OTHER DAY, WOULD RESULT IN AN IMMEDIATE EXECUTION. BUT TODAY IT BRINGS A SHOUT OF SUPPORT. THE MEN ARE IN THIS FOR *EACH OTHER*, AND THE EMPIRE BE FRAGGED.

THEN THE SPEARS BEGIN TO FALL AMONG THEM.

BUT THE DEATHS OF THEIR COMRADES, RATHER THAN INSPIRE FEAR OR DESPAIR --

-- FIRES THE DEFENDERS WITH A FURY TO REDOUBLE THEIR EFFORTS.

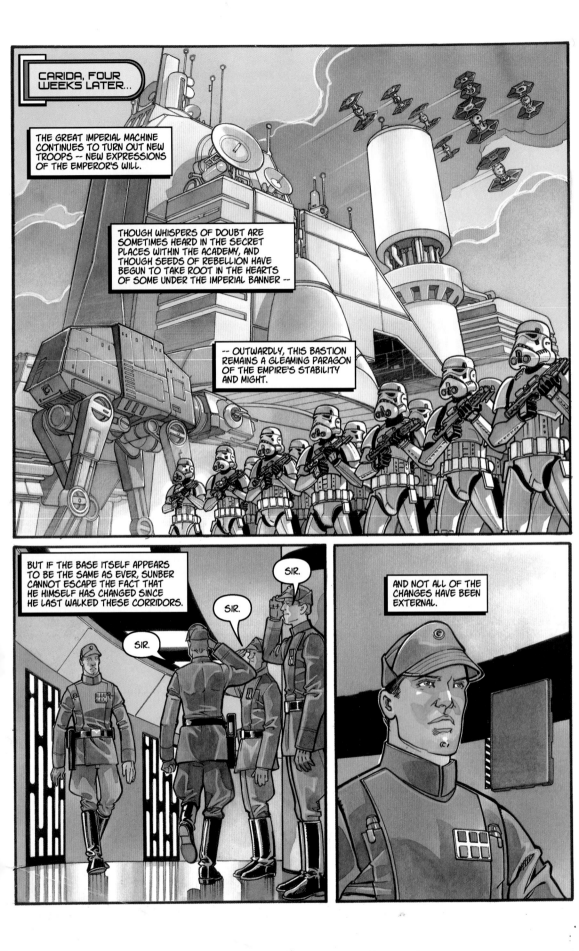

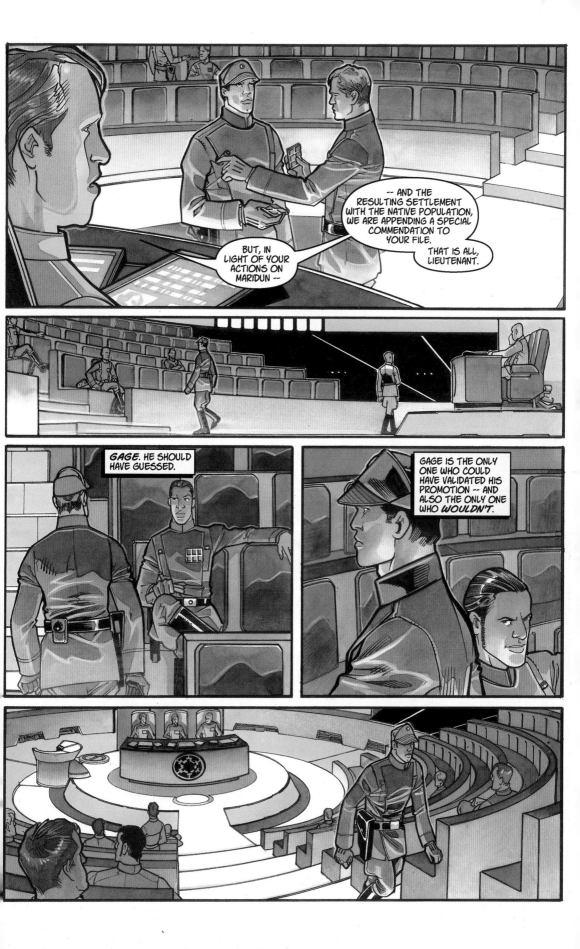

BRIAN CHING
COLORS MICHAEL ATIYEH

TARGET: VADER

SCRIPT RON MARZ
ART BRIAN CHING
COLORS MICHAEL ATIYEH